Reflections
of an
Hispanic
Mennonite

Reflections of an Hispanic Mennonite

José Ortíz and David Graybill

a Budding Tree title

Good Books
Main Street, Intercourse, PA 17534

Acknowledgments

The excerpt in Chapter 9 is reprinted with permission from *Festival Quarterly* magazine, and Chapters 10, 12, 14 and 16 originally appeared there in different form.

Cover by Cheryl Benner
Cover photo by Jonathan Charles
Design by Dawn Ranck

© 1989 by Good Books, Intercourse, PA 17534
International Standard Book Number: 0-934672-78-4
Library of Congress Catalog Card Number: 89-11872

Library of Congress Cataloging-in-Publication Data

Ortiz, José, 1939 –
   Reflections of an Hispanic Mennonite/Jose Ortiz and David Graybill.
     p.   cm.
   ISBN 0-934672-78-4: $6.95
   1. Ortiz, Jose, 1939 –   . 2. Hispanic American Mennonites —
Biography. I. Graybill, David. 1956 –   II. Title.
BX8143.078A3   1989
289.7'092 — dc20
[B]   89-11872
                                              CIP

Contents

Introduction

This is a story about the making of a Christian minister and teacher. In many ways, it is a personal story—an account of my choices, struggles and dreams as I tried to be faithful to the call of God.

But my story is not mine alone. It is a part of many larger stories: the story of my times, of my homeland of Puerto Rico and of the North American society in which I live. More than this, it is a story of two peoples—Hispanics and Mennonites—and how they have challenged one another and the larger world.

Because my story is both individual and corporate, my editors and I have chosen to present it in the form of a conversation. David Graybill and I will alternate chapters, sometimes telling different parts of the story and sometimes describing the same events from different angles.

As a child and young adult, I never expected to be an author. I began writing partly because of the double barrier I face in speaking English: I have both an accent and a speech impediment.

More importantly, I have felt the Holy Spirit calling, "Write!", as John was called in Revelation 14:13. Like the biblical writers, who left us essays, drama, poetry, songs, prophecy, biographies, theological treatises and letters, I feel the need to tell what God has done.

In these chapters, I pay tribute to the missionary effort of the church in years past. Thanks to mission workers, I and many other people came to knowledge of the Christian faith and attended Bible school, college and seminary. Though not without its failures of judgment and sensitivity, the missionary vision is vital to the church. The ability to recruit and retain converts must not be lost.

In addition to the missionary effort, I celebrate Hispanic culture and the 500th anniversary of the coming of Hispanics to the New World in 1492. I celebrate writers such as Gabriel García Márquez and Puerto Rican poet Julia de Burgos, political leaders such as Oscar Arias, and philosophers and human rights advocates such as Adolfo Pérez Esquivel and César Chavez.

Not all of the Hispanic legacy is praiseworthy. I do not celebrate the conquistadores' destruction of native cultures and their taste for the institutional church, nor the development of military governments that oppress their own citizens. I am concerned about the many Hispanics in the United States who suffer from poverty, illiteracy, low self-esteem and other problems. Our culture idealized the señorita, but today there are Hispanic women who have become grandmothers at age 26, and single parenting threatens the extended family pattern.

Lack of formal education is another serious problem. Hispanics conquered a vast continent but are finding it very difficult to conquer the university system. Hispanics make up 8 percent of the U.S. population but only 4 percent of the nation's college students.

To be Hispanic in the United States or Canada is to seek a difficult balance between ethnic pride and the demands of the surrounding culture. For me as a Mennonite, this task is further complicated.

Like Hispanics, Mennonites have a history of separation from the North American mainstream and continue to hold distinctive values. Being Mennonite as well as Hispanic requires me to function in not only two, but three, cultures.

Yet my 37 years in this group of Christians have shaped my identity as well as unsettled it. Anabaptism — the historical tradition to which Mennonites belong — has been crucial in defining my stance on peace, justice, service and the church as a community of faith. Mennonite pastors and teachers have been models for me, both as people and as leaders.

Founded in Switzerland in 1525, the Anabaptist movement was named for its members' practice of baptizing adult believers, even if they had been baptized as children. In the 16th century, Anabaptists were burned at the stake for their beliefs in nonviolence, the priesthood of all believers and the separation of church and state. Today, Anabaptist ideas receive a respectful hearing from Catholic and mainline Protestant groups. Mennonite pastors and administrators, however, often suffer at the hands of their own church members, due to lack of trust, overburdened agendas and low budgets.

Partly because of this, the Mennonite Church faces a leadership shortage. Its ministers are graying, and the denomination's goal of training 100 new pastors a year exceeds the pool of college graduates considering church vocations.

I hope that this book will focus increased attention on the need for effective leaders. I further hope that the book will encourage readers of all backgrounds to reflect on God's work in their lives and in the lives of their congregations and denominations.

Finally, I hope that these chapters will encourage full inclusiveness in the church. Mennonites and other denominations have begun to open leadership roles to women and minorities, but much more remains to be done. I hope for a day when such names as Martínez, Nan Ding, Kedzie and Ortíz are no longer exotic, but commonplace among pastors and church administrators.

—José Ortíz

1.

Growing Up
at Coamo Arriba

On May 3, 1939, four months before Hitler's invasion of Poland, a midwife in the mountains of Puerto Rico delivered the first child of Mariano and María Green de Ortíz. Because the midwife only went to town a few times a month, José's birth was not reported until two weeks later. In order to avoid a fine for the delay, the midwife reported the date of birth as May 15 — the date that still appears on José's driver's license and passport.

The area in which the nine Ortíz children grew up was known as Coamo Arriba, an unincorporated village up river from the town of Coamo. There were no paved roads in the village. Instead, the houses were connected by a network of paths. To get to a neighbor's house, one usually had to walk to another neighbor's house and take a connecting path.

José's father was a farmer who raised corn, beans, oranges, tobacco and lemons. He was a loyal supporter of the Partido Popular, or People's Party, one of Puerto Rico's three main political groups. Though Mariano had not finished high school, José describes him as an articulate man who loved to discuss politics and the Bible.

According to José, his mother was more reserved. Six years older than her husband, María devoted herself to her children and the women of the community.

Her unusual family name — Green — was and re-

13

mains a source of mystery. An uncle of José's speculates that it came from the marriage of an English sailor and a Puerto Rican woman in the distant past.

The members of the Ortíz family were "very close to each other and very close to nature," José recalls. "I felt my father and mother were such loving people. We felt secure, we felt protected."

As a child, José enjoyed baseball, swimming and exploring, sometimes alone and sometimes with his brothers and sisters. He was especially fond of Elena, who was five years younger.

In addition to playing, José helped to take produce to town and to care for the family's horses and cows. He carried wood and water for his parents and harvested coffee for hire.

"I would say I began to work earlier than the average child today," he says. "But that was country living."

As a result of being given responsibility, "I am not surprised by new people, new situations or thunderstorms," he continues. "Sometimes I believe my kids are deprived. Deprived of nature, deprived because we let them stay in their childhood so long."

Happy though his early years were, José felt an urge to discover the world beyond Coamo Arriba. He remembers learning to read at about the time that Mao Tse-tung was coming to power and seeing the headline "Guerra en China" (War in China). José became a voracious reader of newspapers, textbooks and comic books—"whatever I could get ahold of." He read and re-read the few books available at home, including a book of Greek mythology and a home medical guide.

("It's very disappointing today," he says. "There are so many books available, and people just don't read.")

Because the local elementary school was an hour's walk from home, José's father kept him out of school until he was seven—a year older than many of his classmates. As the oldest child in the family, José had no brothers or sisters to take care of him, and Mariano wanted to make sure that his son could avoid the bulls that roamed the field between the Ortíz house and the school.

José more than made up for the lost time. He skipped fifth grade and completed junior high school in two years, delighting his father, who wanted him to become a teacher.

When José entered junior high, he moved to the home of an uncle in another village. He commuted to his parents' house on weekends, walking two or three hours each way.

"I was ready to leave home," José says. "I wouldn't be happy staying in one place. I enjoy forming new relationships, learning to know new communities."

On the other hand, José admits that dividing his time between two places had a price. Junior high "is the time when you're forming networks," he points out. What he gained in breadth of friendships he lost in depth, he says.

During his last few years of elementary school, José became acquainted with an unlikely group of people— Mennonite mission workers from the U.S. mainland. The Mennonites, who were pacifists and ethnically German, had come to Puerto Rico to establish clinics, agriculture programs and churches.

Because he came from a poor family, José did not feel at home in the local Catholic church. The mass, in those days before Vatican II, was in a foreign language. The priest kept company with the rich people. He drove a black Lincoln Continental with a dog in the back seat and refused to give rides to the people he passed along the road.

15

The Mennonites José met were different—friendly, unassuming and willing to reach across boundaries of class and culture. "If Mennonites came by in a jeep, they would pick you up," he recalls. "They could always fit in one more."

José attended summer Bible school classes sponsored by the Mennonites. "Around 1950" he began attending Sunday and Wednesday night services at the Mennonite church of Smirna de Coamo Arriba, a half hour's walk from home. But, José says, it was the Mennonite summer camp progams that left the most lasting impression on him. One of those sessions, when he was 13 years old, changed the course of his life.

2.

Grace by the River

My walk of faith began in the summer of 1952 when I responded to a simple chalk talk. Surrounded by 70 young campers at a YMCA camp at El Yunque, I heard a speaker talk about the narrow gate that leads to eternal life and the wide gate that leads to life without God (Matthew 7:13). Each person needs to decide which doorway to enter, the speaker said. I responded by raising my hand and accepting Jesus as savior.

I had been reached by the transcendent God. With my head down, I walked to my cabin, stopping on the way at a light pole, which I circled several times.

I have not felt the same feeling again, not even when I got married or was ordained as a minister of the Word. Conversion as I experienced it is an overpowering event in which the new self is freed from time and space. Yet, paradoxically, that self must abide within a body of flesh and bones that is subject to temptation. Grace enables us both to start our journey of faith and to continue it when we fail.

It took me four days to share my feelings with my father, not because I doubted my decision but because I respected him and was afraid that he would disapprove. Also, I wanted him to know that I had made up my mind and was not simply caught up in the enthusiasm of the moment.

I was the first in my family to join an evangelical group. Like many people in Puerto Rico, our family upheld the Roman Catholic faith in a nominal way. When one of my brothers was seriously ill as an infant, the priest came on horseback, through heavy rains, and baptized him. In after-school sessions, I learned the basics of preparation for first communion, though I never participated in the mass. Because of the Latin language and the large crowds, I stayed on the fringes when the priest came to our community, though I admired the liturgy, images and impressive buildings of the church.

As a non-practicing Catholic, I had known little of the biblical story. Now, as a new believer, I immersed myself in the New Testament. Luke's gospel and the chronicles of Acts were so crispy, so fresh. The poetry of John was a delicacy, the symbolism of Matthew hard to stomach. Paul's letters were colored with adventure, while Revelation gave the impression that it was for adult readers only.

I wish I could recapture that excitement about the Word of God again. Now I have built an alarm system that alerts me to Greek ideas, Jewish symbols and gnostic influences and sees how the Word has been interpreted through the eyes of various church traditions. Useful as these skills are, however, there is a time to simply say, "I believe; the scriptures can be trusted."

When I look back on my conversion, I see a specific time and place. Other people, who grew up in the church, see conversion as a process, like the accumulation of growth rings in an oak tree. In some cases, people who experienced this sort of conversion bloom spiritually; in other cases, they fall away, forgetting that one must be a child of God, not a grandchild.

For me, however, that evening at El Yunque is an experience to be remembered and shared, just as Kunta Kinte in *Roots* told his children of those events carved forever in his memory. I have often taken my family to visit El Yunque. While my children enjoy the river, I look at the cabins and meeting hall, find the pole I circled, and let my mind replay that event more than 30 years ago. When the boys come back, I tell them, "This is the place where I decided to become a Christian."

Before concluding my pastorate at the Summit Hills church in San Juan, I returned to the river with a group of young people. Several of them were baptized there amid singing, tears and hugs. For them, as for me, this camp in eastern Puerto Rico is more than a rain forest and mountainside. It is a place where we felt the touch of God.

3.

Becoming a Pastor

José did not choose to become a pastor, so much as circumstances chose him.

During José's youth, missionaries often had responsibilities with more than one congregation. It was common for a mission worker to preach at one church on Sunday morning and another in the afternoon, or at different churches on different weeks.

Lester Hershey, the pastor of the Smirna congregation, couldn't be at church every week, so he asked José to help with the preaching. He also encouraged him to assist in visitation of members.

"By the age of 19 I had been in the pulpit," José recalls. "It was done not because of my gifts but out of the church's need."

The experiment could have failed badly. Not only had the members of the church known José from childhood, but the group now included his parents, brothers and sisters, who had begun attending after his conversion.

"I was worried that the church wouldn't respect me, because I was one of the neighbor kids," José says. Instead, "the people were very helpful."

Even so, José had no plans to make the ministry a career. He applied to the University of Puerto Rico in 1957, with plans to study nursing, but was turned down despite his strong academic record.

"So one afternoon Lester Hershey said, 'Why not spend a year at Bible school?'"

The idea was new, but José responded eagerly. It was a chance to continue his studies, to see a new place and to meet new people.

"I liked what I'd seen of Mennonites," he says. "They had nice basketball courts, nice trimmed lawns and smooth-running tractors. The women were pretty."

La Plata, where the Bible school was located, was less than 40 miles from José's home community. But getting there, before Puerto Rico's industrialization, was an adventure.

The trip required a horseback ride, a walk and two rides by bus or private vehicle. José would go to the road and wait for a *público* or a car that had an empty seat. The entire journey took half a day.

"I used to have Sunday morning service, and then I would have to run to be back in La Plata for school the next morning," José recalls. "It was exciting and exhausting."

Though he had enrolled in the school without a vocational goal in mind, José found himself drawn to church leadership. After his first two years at La Plata, the school closed. But José went on to study Bible at Hesston College in Kansas and Goshen College, a Mennonite school in northern Indiana.

After earning a bachelor's degree from Goshen, he returned to Puerto Rico in 1962 and pastored a congregation in La Cuchilla, where he met his wife, Iraida.

("She was a good Sunday school superintendent and I was a minister. So we merged," José says, with typical brevity.)

José studied at Eastern Baptist Theological Seminary in Philadelphia from 1967–69, and was pastor of the Summit Hills congregation from 1970–74. He earned a doctorate of ministry degree from McCormick Theological Seminary in Chicago in 1979, and was interim pastor of the New Holland Spanish Mennonite Church in New Holland, Pennsylvania, in 1983.

Although José says he has learned from people in each of these settings, he cites two teachers at the La Plata school as among his most important models for pastoral leadership.

Angel Luis Gutierrez "used to read *Time* magazine and the Bible together," José recalls. "He was so gifted in preaching contemporary issues."

John Driver, a Mennonite missionary, pastor and writer, showed José how to "present the Word in a compassionate way."

Like his mentors, José believes that there is more to being a pastor than knowing the right theology or proper leadership techniques. Just as important, he says, is "the touch of the Spirit"—the ability to help people feel the presence of God in their lives.

In worship, the minister must "provide the wine" that gives the congregation strength for the coming week, José believes. Too often, "people come seeking bread and wine, and they get stones or hay."

On an even more basic level, he says, the pastor must be present at times of trouble, sickness and death. Offering support in these situations is better than trying to provide answers, José believes.

While he was in San Juan, José officiated at the funeral of a man in his mid-forties who had been shot. Though the man was not a member of the Summit Hills church, his children attended the school run by the congregation and were playmates of José's children.

"There are some things we cannot explain," José recalls saying at the funeral. "In spite of this, in the midst of this," he told the bereaved family, "God is the sustainer of life. As you go from here in tears, God goes with you to help you put your life back together."

In addition to comforting families and individuals in sorrow, José has sometimes shared the joy as people who have suffered loss experience spiritual healing. The first funeral José conducted was for a 26-year-old woman who died of cancer. Later, he officiated at the wedding when her husband remarried.

"It was kind of a Chapter 2 in his life," José says.

While preaching and administration are important, "The most important role of the pastor is to pour oil on the hurts of the people," José believes. "If you do that, the rest falls into place."

4.
Going to La Plata for Bible School

The call to the ministry for the apostle Paul was an event in living color with sound effects. Not so my call to attend Bible school.

I landed at the Mennonite Bible Institute in La Plata because the University of Puerto Rico turned me down. I was not the son of a politician nor the child of a wealthy family, and in those days the major criterion for entering the university was not academic performance or professional potential but having the right *palanca,* or connections.

Bible school was hardly a glamorous place. There were only three full-time teachers, all of whom had part-time pastorates or were involved in Christian education, and a dozen students. Classes were held in the morning, with afternoons reserved for working at part-time jobs in order to support ourselves. In the evenings we had supervised study time. During the weekend we preached, taught Sunday school and did home visitation in different congregations.

Because of the scarcity of funds we worked; because of the scarcity of pastors we preached and ministered; because of the scarcity of time we commuted between assignments with a prayer in our hearts, new concepts in our brains and required reading in our hands. Because of scarcity we developed strong backbones and determination.

The affluent society tends to generate a cushioned faith, a low-calorie gospel, and leaves no room for the miracle to happen. In the Bible miracles occur in times of stress and scarcity, never in periods of surplus. I don't romanticize the past, nor poverty, nor scarcity, but those who survive the trials of limitation tend to be assertive in any type of enterprise.

Paul spent three years in solitude in Samaria; I spent two years in learning activity in La Plata, commuting from the church-home to the Mennonite Hospital, where I worked as an office clerk, maintenance man and, at times, a chaplain.

Yet I, like Paul, was sent where I was for a purpose. Going to La Plata, where the Mennonites had been established for 12 years, was like walking into a sunrise. There was activity on the farm, in the shops, the park, at the dorms — everywhere. The whole community was experiencing a renaissance.

With the Mennonites had come new possibilities and a new outlook. The Mennonites were not in a rush to turn water into wine, but they turned the tobacco barn into a hospital and taught local people who had limited technical skills how to drive tractors, vaccinate chickens, take blood pressures and do a series of jobs never thought of.

They also brought new ideas. As Bible students, we were introduced to such exotic terms as "exegesis" and "homiletics," as well as how to outline three-part sermons with the assistance of Bible commentaries, concordances and dictionaries.

The Mennonites can even be credited with bringing Handel's *Messiah* to La Plata! The evening I first heard it is still vivid in my mind. There was a lingering sunset in the valley. Suddenly the quietness was interrupted by the sound of blasting trumpets and the echoes of voices singing "Aleluhia, Aleluhia!" Like a man possessed I left the study hall of Casa Grande and began to look at the clouds, expecting to see angels and the return of the Lord. After some prolonged heartbeats, I realized that the music was coming from a local church. Once again the Mennonites had done a new thing, and like John on the island of Patmos I almost fell to my feet.

During my stay at La Plata, I learned two basic principles that have helped me through my adult life. First, you work or develop programs with the resources that you have on hand. The Mennonites, known for being barn raisers, chose not to erect a building but to use one that was already there. Instead of importing more missionaries and Bible teachers from their colleges and seminaries, they trained local people; instead of bringing in food from Pennsylvania or Florida, they opted to raise crops and animals locally.

By taking this approach, they validated local resources and people. Rather than tie people to their past and their limitations, Jesus' style of ministry was to provide options and ask people where they wanted to go. The Mennonites followed this example. As a result of their investment, struggling tobacco farmers became successful chicken raisers, and unskilled janitors got skilled positions as cooks and nurses aides.

A second principle that the Mennonites of La Plata taught me was to be assertive and determined. Assertiveness comes out of a clear assessment of the circumstances and the feeling that you have been empowered and authorized to act on behalf of others. Empowerment is a gift of the Spirit.

When local commitment, assertiveness and empowerment come together, as they did at La Plata, remarkable things can happen. Today a simple diploma from that school hangs on my office wall next to several others from graduate schools. Together they give witness to the mustard seed effect.

5.

Journeys North and South

When the La Plata Bible school closed in 1959, John Driver suggested that José attend Hesston College, a Mennonite junior college in south-central Kansas. Driver, a Hesston College graduate, thought the school would be a good place for his student to enter the U.S. educational world and the North American Mennonite community.

Under the direction of professor John Koppenhaver, a former missionary in Argentina, the college was inviting Hispanic students. With a student body of less than 300, Hesston offered a relaxed environment with relatively little prejudice.

José recalls few encounters with racism during his two years at the college. One of these occurred off campus, when he went to a museum in Kansas City and didn't eat in the cafeteria because a black Hispanic was along. ("They had art from all over the world, but they couldn't show the art of living," he says.)

At Hesston, José's biggest problems were the language and the climate.

"I was familiar with written English," he says. "But when it came to oral English, it was difficult. Today, there are all kinds of services and tutoring. Then, you were on your own."

Although he had grown up in the tropics, José also found it hard to adjust to the scorching summers on the plains. Unlike his home in the mountains, the wind brought no cooling and there was little shade.

"The first day in Hesston, it was so hot I took five showers," he recalls.

John Koppenhaver could not change the weather, but he did what he could to make José feel at home. José remembers him as "a happy person," who was willing to go to great lengths for his students.

Koppenhaver saw to it that José's education didn't stop at the edge of campus. Thanks to his help, José made connections with Hispanics in neighboring communities and traveled widely during school vacations.

José helped in a Baptist mission in Wichita and visited another Baptist group in Hutchinson, Kansas. He met Mexican Mennonites in Texas, Illinois and Iowa and helped in an effort to start a church in Pico Rivera, California, near Whittier. After his graduation from Hesston (with a two-year, associates degree), he visited an aunt in Milwaukee, then spent the summer in New York City, working at the Mennonite House of Friendship and as an animal lab caretaker at Sloan-Kettering Research Center.

Through his travels, he became aware for the first time of his Puerto Rican identity in relation to other Hispanics.

"Being a Puerto Rican, it was hard for people to place me," he says. "In a sense, I have a unique opportunity. I can play the Hispanic card. But, like Paul, who had the advantage of Roman citizenship, I have the benefits of being a U.S. citizen."

Such a dual identity also has drawbacks, he points out. Because Puerto Ricans can easily return home, they "have been a group that has lived two realities — living on the mainland but longing for the island." As a result, they do not fully commit themselves to their new environment. "The price of choice is instability in both places."

In the fall of 1961, José enrolled at Goshen College in Indiana. Though he was only at Goshen for a year, he completed requirements for a B.A. in Bible and learned to know Hispanics in Chicago and the Goshen community. Following his graduation the next summer, he and his roommate, Stanley Heatwole, traveled through Mexico, Central America and Venezuela.

José and Stanley planned to drive a friend's car to Texas. When the vehicle broke down at St. Joseph, Missouri, they took a flight to Mexico City and traveled to Panama City by bus.

"Those were the days when you could travel freely in Central America without fear," José observes. "Not anymore."

José and Stanley flew from Panama to Venezuela, then to Puerto Rico. They parted company, and José spent several days with his parents, who had moved to the town of Aibonito. The next week, he began teaching third grade at the Betania Mennonite Academy in Pulgillas and serving as part-time pastor at La Cuchilla.

As José notes, August was "an explosive month." In addition to moving and starting two new jobs, he became acquainted with Iraida Rivera, whom he married the following May.

Like José, Iraida had lived on the mainland. She was bilingual and active in the church. Her home community was next to his.

Dating a local woman raised the eyebrows of some members, but José survived their questions and overcame the skepticism of Iraida's mother.

Following the couple's wedding, José channeled his energy into church work and further education. The La Chuchilla church merged with the Palo Hincado congregation in Barranquitas, and José became a full-time pastor. Pursuing an interest that had been encouraged by Elvin Snyder, the Bible school director, he enrolled in an Hispanic literature program at the Inter American University of Puerto Rico. (He completed 30 hours of course work, but left without a degree.)

In 1965, Rolando Ortíz was born, the first of José and Iraida's three children. The family might have remained in Puerto Rico, but for two events. First, the church José was pastoring ran out of money to pay a full-time salary, forcing him to get a job as a social worker. Then, in June of 1966, José went into the bathroom one morning and doubled over with pain. Iraida helped him up and into the family's Volkswagen. That night, José underwent an emergency appendectomy at the nearby Mennonite hospital.

José had been working himself to exhaustion as a caseworker during the week, a university student on Saturday mornings, a pastor and a father. He had no medical insurance. After two days in the hospital, most of his savings were gone. He was angry that the church did not provide for his need and humiliated that he had so little money to fall back on.

"I made up my mind to leave everything," he says.

José resigned from the church. His brother Héctor had been a migrant worker in New Jersey and was interested in going back. So José decided to travel with him to Philadelphia, ahead of their families. At the last minute, Héctor changed his mind, so José flew by himself to New York. He took a train to 30th Street Station in Philadelphia and a taxi to the YMCA hotel.

"I came to Philadelphia not knowing where I was going," he says. "The next day when I opened the window and saw the highrises, I was almost choked."

José ate breakfast and bought a map of the city. To his

31

amazement, he found that the address of a person he wanted to contact was within walking distance.

"When I got there, the lady was in front of the door, like she was waiting for someone to arrive," he says.

Juanita Torres gave José a temporary home and helped him find an apartment for himself and his family. She also helped him find his way to Eastern Baptist Theological Seminary, which had been recommended to him by a friend who learned that José was going to Philadelphia.

Iraida and Rolando came a month later, along with José's sister Consuelo. The family moved into an apartment at 16th and Green Streets, in one of the few parts of the city in which both blacks and Hispanics lived. José got a job with a company that made laboratory equipment and enrolled at the seminary.

During their second year in the city, José and Iraida helped to start a Voluntary Service unit of the General Conference Mennonite Church. The couple moved to a neighborhood northeast of Temple University and served as houseparents to four young volunteers, who were assisting in a city church.

José and Iraida's second child, Ricardo, was born in 1968, and the family moved to the seminary campus. José juggled his classwork and a variety of part-time jobs. For a brief time, he held four jobs at once. He worked as a gardener, did substitute teaching, put a handicapped person to bed and was part-time Bible teacher at Second Mennonite Church, now a black congregation, at Franklin Street and Indiana Avenue.

After José received a master of arts degree in May 1969, the Ortíz family returned to Puerto Rico. In doing so, he and Iraida turned down a chance to enter urban ministry in Newark, New Jersey, and for José to enroll in a doctoral program at Rutgers University.

José (front row, right) listens as John Driver teaches a class at the La Plata Bible School in Puerto Rico.

José receives his ministerial license from Addona Nissley, secretary of the Puerto Rican Mennonite conference, in a service at Betania in March 1957. Looking on (from left to right) are conference representatives Samuel Rolón, Fidel Santiago and Melquiades Santiago.

Lester T. Hershey officiates at the marriage of José and Iraida on May 31, 1963. "On the day of the wedding, I worked most of the morning at the Betania school. Royal Snyder, one of the teachers, loaned me his car so I could go to town for a haircut and to do some last-minute errands."

José poses with his students on graduation day at Betania in May 1964. Among the class members are two of his brothers. José Luis (third row, second from left) is now deceased. Alfredo (third row right, wearing glasses) runs the Ortíz family farm in Asomante with his father, Mariano.

Family portrait in August 1974. Ronaldo is at far left, Rolando in the center and Ricardo at far right.

José in Alajuela, Costa Rica, with Armando Hernández (center) and Raúl Rosado. "The occasion was a meeting of Latin American representatives of the Mennonite conferences involved in radio ministry under Mennonite Broadcasts, now Mennonite Media Ministries."

José preaches at the New Holland Spanish Mennonite Church in Pennsylvania, where he was interim pastor for six months in 1983. "Little did I know that Juanita Rolón [second from left, front row] would be our secretary in the Hispanic Ministries department at the college, or that Noel Santiago [center, beside her] would sit on the Hispanic coordinating council as a Mennonite Board of Missions administrator. A year after this photo was taken, they got married and enrolled at Goshen."

Instead, the family was without income for two months, before José began his teaching job at the Mennonite school associated with the Summit Hills church. He and Iraida "still wonder" if going back to the island was the right move, he admits. "Those are the 'what ifs.'"

At the end of 1969, José applied for a pastoral position at a Mennonite congregation in another part of the island. But he was turned down when he demanded that he be paid the same amount as a missionary would be.

"I was a young turk," José says. "Missionaries were well paid, and they had less formal education than I did."

Meanwhile, the Summit Hills church had asked José to chair the committee that planned worship services. José said he would—if his family could live in the parsonage. The arrangement worked so well that the church invited José to become its pastor, first on a part-time and then on a full-time basis.

José's five years at Summit Hills were happy ones, both personally and in the church. Iraida gave birth to their youngest son, Ronaldo. José grew in pastoral ability, and the church grew in membership and expanded its outreach.

"We have a saying in Spanish: 'The congregation makes the pastor,'" José observes. "Those people were very good to me."

The Summit Hills church "had all kinds of resources," he continues. "There was money. There were professionals with all sorts of skills. There were aggressive youth."

It was at Summit Hills, José says, that he saw the need for good organization in the church. A member of the congregation helped him to buy two army surplus file

cabinets. Guillermo Ramirez Sr. and Arcadio Qui-
ñones, members who were government engineers,
showed him how to administer programs and to set
goals.

In addition to overseeing day-to-day projects, José
used his sharpened organizational skills to plan three
trips outside the island. With the help of the Evangelical
Council, an umbrella group for evangelicals in Puerto
Rico, he organized a visit by members of the Summit
Hills youth group to migrant workers on the U.S. main-
land. In addition, he helped the church send a gospel
team to Central America and led a group of Puerto
Rican Mennonites on a visit to Mennonites in the
United States and Canada.

José's years at the church were not without problems.
The biggest difficulty, he says, was trying to deal re-
sponsibly with the Mennonite volunteers who came to
Puerto Rico. Though some showed a high level of
maturity, he says, others were young people primarily
interested in a vacation in the sun, away from their
home churches and communities. Along with this, José
felt he was not respected by the Anglo administrators of
the volunteer program.

Still, as 1973 drew to a close, José could look back
with satisfaction on five productive years for himself
and the congregation. Summit Hills was thriving. Yet
somehow he felt restless, anxious for a change.

In Washington, Vice President Spiro Agnew had
resigned. Within eight months, a President too would
be forced from office, and José would make another
journey north.

6.

The Crossroads
at Villa Caparra

Villa Caparra in northern Puerto Rico was
founded by Juan Ponce De León in 1508, 17 years
before the birth of Anabaptism in Europe. Today
the ruins of the original town lie behind iron gates,
with New York-style, high-rise apartment buildings mushrooming in the background. In a sense,
Villa Caparra stands between the Spanish conquistadores of Puerto Rico's past and the island's future
tied to the United States.

My route home each day from San Juan to Baya-
mon took me through Villa Caparra. One afternoon I had an uneasy feeling as I reflected on the
busy day past and the church meeting planned for
that evening. While waiting for the traffic light to
turn green, I surprised myself by whispering a question: "Lord, it's been five years like this. Can I do
something else?"

Several months passed before a letter arrived
from Mac Bustos, president of the Concilio Nacional, the Council of Hispanic Mennonite
Churches in the United States. "Will you be a candidate for the position of Associate Secretary for
Hispanic Concerns?" the letter asked. After reading the letter several times, I realized that three
other, well qualified candidates were also being
considered. "Let them be the first options," I

thought. "I will wait." So I did not respond by the requested date.

During this time, however, I began to recall my Christmas visits in Pico Rivera and Los Angeles, where I served in a Spanish mission with Richard and Luella Fahndrich. I also recalled the Sunday meetings with a Mexican Baptist group in Hutchinson, Kansas, and my visit to Premont, Texas (where I was introduced to *tamales*), on another Christmas vacation while I was studying at Hesston College.

The Easter season when we visited with the Zapata family in Davenport, Iowa, and they became Christians, the summer in New York City with the Mennonite House of Friendship, and gospel team tours to Chicago and the Mennonite community of Archbold, Ohio, also came to my mind.

Mac Bustos, I recalled, was a brother to Mario Bustos, whom I had helped when he was a pastor in Milwaukee.

I remembered working in a Spanish mission in Milford, Indiana, 12 miles south of Goshen, while a student at Goshen College. I thought of the month I had spent selling Christian literature to Hispanics in the Quad Cities in 1962, and of my return to Puerto Rico afterward by way of Mexico, Central America and Caracas, Venezuela. Perhaps the Lord had prepared me through these experiences for a larger task.

The phone call came early one afternoon while I was at the church office. Lupe De León on behalf of the Concilio told me to "send in the application, pronto." That led to an interview at a motel in Rosemont, Illinois, and a job offer.

Once again our family began to plan for a trip to *el norte*. My prayer at the traffic light had been

answered, yet I had many questions. How to inter-
pret our departure to the Summit Hills congregation? Was I on short-term loan to the mainland, a
missionary to the sending church or a prophet
going into exile? Would I be happy trading my
pulpit for a desk and worship services for business
meetings — especially among Mennonites, who
spent hours chasing consensus?

Disengagement from the Summit Hills church
was painful. The church council had been in-
formed of my trip to the States and the reason
behind it. Still, it was not easy to leave when the
church was growing and outreach projects were
beginning in the towns of Cataño and Country
Club.

In addition, the children were not sure they
wanted to live in Chicago. Their fears were not
relieved by our introduction to the city on a blister-
ing summer day. We drove a rented van from Cleve-
land, past the smokestacks of Gary, Indiana, and
onto the Day Ryan Expressway, the world's busiest
road. Fortunately, a phone call to Ron Collins,
pastor of Lawndale Mennonite Church, helped us
find our way around the confusing cloverleaf exits
to his home on the West Side, where we would
spend the first week.

In August 1974, on the week that Richard Nixon
resigned as president of the United States, I began
work in an office complex next to O'Hare International Airport. I was given a job description, some
file space, yellow pads, a credit card and a dictating
machine (which I never used), along with a word of
welcome, a prayer and several statements that
amounted to, "You are on your own; if you need any
help, don't hesitate to ask."

41

7.

Guiding, Speaking and Dreaming

José's eight years as a Mennonite Church administrator were eventful ones, even by his own energetic standards.

As associate secretary, it was José's job to represent the needs and concerns of Hispanic Mennonites to the rest of the denomination. This involved a wide variety of tasks. He reported regularly to both the Hispanic Concilio and the Mennonite Church General Board. He took part in committee meetings. He wrote Sunday school materials and articles for church magazines. He preached sermons and spoke at the 1975 General Assembly at Eureka, Illinois, one of the denomination's biennial conventions. He listened, advised and made proposals.

José's position put him at the center of historic changes in the Mennonite Church. Hispanic congregations were growing at an astonishing rate. Black and Spanish-speaking members were demanding a greater role in setting the church's direction. Young Anglos were starting to discover the city.

For José, the period was one of personal changes as well. He and Iraida bought their first house. The Ortíz family moved from Chicago to suburban Lombard to Goshen, Indiana. And José earned a doctor of ministry degree from McCormick seminary and a master's degree in public administration from Indiana University.

José recalls the years in Illinois as exceptionally good ones for his family. The children were "young enough to be flexible," he says, and adapted well to their new surroundings.

The Ortíz boys found the city full of discoveries. Ricardo had never seen a Protestant pastor who wore vestments, until his first day at a Lutheran elementary school. He came home and told his father, "This morning I saw God."

Not every adjustment was easy for the family. In Puerto Rico, the Ortízes lived in a house with four bedrooms, two bathrooms and a patio. In Chicago, they tried to make do in a cramped third-floor apartment that had only one heater and no heat in the bathroom.

Maria Snyder, who had met José at Hesston, saw the apartment and thought the family deserved better. She went to Ivan Kauffmann, a staff member for General Board who later became general secretary of the Mennonite Church.

Kauffmann was a former moderator of the local district body, Illinois Mennonite Conference. At his urging, the conference loaned money for a down payment, so that the Ortízes could buy a house in Lombard, the town to which José's office had been moved.

The experience of finding housing was "just one expression of the old pietistic word 'trust,'" José says. "I have respect for the Illinois Mennonite Conference," he adds, "because when I needed them they were there."

Although he enjoyed living in Lombard, José came to feel that it was a backwater as far as his work was concerned. True, the general secretary's office was there, along with the office of Mennonite World Conference. But these employed less than a dozen people together. Most of the Mennonite Church offices — including four of the denomination's five program boards—were in northern Indiana.

In 1977 the General Board accepted José's proposal to move his office from Lombard to Elkhart. José and Iraida were able to sell their house in less than a week. They made enough money from the sale to pay off the loan and buy a house in Goshen.

A tree-lined town of some 20,000 people, Goshen proved to be "a dream community to raise kids," José says. Yet the family experienced prejudice as well.

When one of the boys was sick, José phoned a local doctor to set an appointment. The receptionist heard his accent and demanded payment in cash. Later, when Iraida said that José worked "at the Greencroft Center," the same person asked if he was a maintenance man.

An Anglo family that moved in next to the Ortízes got a Welcome Wagon visit. It seemed more than chance that José and Iraida never did.

Choosing which church to attend posed a different problem. While living in Lombard, the family had made a point of driving 25 miles back to the city to attend an Hispanic congregation. In Goshen, the pastor of the only Hispanic Mennonite church had a fifth grade education. José had a doctorate.

In spite of this and an abundance of Anglo Mennonite churches in the area, the Ortízes became active in the Hispanic group. According to José, the family's years with the congregation—Iglesia del Buen Pastor, or Good Shepherd Mennonite Church—have been good ones. Anything the church may have lacked in content, it has "made up for in relationships," he says. People in the congregation have been "aunts and uncles, even grandmothers and grandfathers, for our children."

José's frustrations with Good Shepherd have had less to do with theological depth than with organization and planning, he continues. Because of his experience and training, José sees program implications that other members sometimes do not, he says.

By the end of 1981, José's varied activities were wearing him down. In addition to congregational and work responsibilities, he was teaching part-time at Goshen College and studying for his degree in public administration.

"I was beginning to feel pain in my back," he recalls. "I didn't want to carry more suitcases through airports or sit through meetings."

There were family pressures: Iraida said the boys needed José. In addition, José felt frustrated with what he saw as a needlessly complicated denominational structure and with his role in it. District conferences kept their distance from Hispanic congregations, José believed. Conference leaders seldom involved themselves in problems affecting a Spanish-speaking church, but called José and the Hispanic Concilio to put out the fire.

Early in 1982 José submitted his resignation, to be effective at the end of the summer.

José left with mixed feelings about the Mennonite Church. On one hand, he was grateful for the warmth with which he was received by individuals and at church gatherings. He appreciated the willingness of the church to support his graduate study, by allowing him to work a flexible schedule and providing professional development funds.

José also had high regard for Kauffmann and Paul Kraybill, the two general secretaries with whom he worked. Kraybill, who became executive secretary of Mennonite World Conference, showed José how to organize people and events. Kauffmann, who succeeded Kraybill, impressed José with his "patience and stewardship." Several times, Kauffmann repaired the duplicating machine in the office himself, as a way to avoid expensive service calls.

On the other hand, José wondered why Anglo Mennonites had so many meetings and made decisions so slowly. He was frustrated with their clannishness and emphasis on tradition, and tired of people who couldn't spell his name or understand his culture.

Anglo Mennonites had been outsiders themselves in North American society, yet they found it hard to welcome other outsiders to their group.

"Where we stand, Anglo Mennonites used to stand," José reflected. "But some people have forgotten."

8.

Working for the Concilio Nacional

Perhaps the greatest strength I brought to my work with the Concilio Nacional was naivete. When I began the job, I was unaware of many of the issues I would face.

The first was leadership style. Unlike Anglo Mennonites, who tend to be uncomfortable with strong leaders, Hispanics have been conditioned to hold structures and administrators in high regard. Thus, in coming to the Concilio and the General Board, I thought I was coming to the holy of holies where Mennonite Church policies were made. Once there, however, I was kindly told that policy was shaped in congregations, at "the grassroots level." Sometimes I believed it, sometimes I doubted. At times, I felt that the refusal to exercise power was a tactic to avoid responsibility — a game that Hubert Brown, a black Mennonite administrator, calls "Anabaptist volleyball."

In addition, I discovered that Hispanics and Anglos had very different feelings about my position. Hispanics looked at the Concilio and the associate secretary's office with high expectations, while Mennonites of non-minority background were uneasy. Both groups, I found, lacked a clear picture of where my position fit in the maze of church agencies and acronyms.

Sometimes I was burned, sometimes I learned. I felt keenly the need to present the image of an efficient manager, both to provide a model for Hispanics and to break the cultural stereotypes held by some Anglos. Partly for this reason, I made a point of being on time for work and keeping clear records. At the same time, I tried to maintain a personal touch and to answer mail the same day it arrived.

Along with the responsibilities and struggles of my job came many joys. Because Hispanic Mennonites tended to be first-generation believers, they had enthusiasm for evangelism and church growth. Their commitment was to the future, not the past.

They expressed the Christian faith with exuberance, and saw the Christian life in the energetic terms of the Book of Acts. They had a feeling of being God's people on a march to heaven, since "this world is not our home."

Hispanic pastors were developing congregations that emphasized salvation and charismatic preaching. They found Hispanics as a group responsive to the evangelical message when it was presented within the context of Latin culture.

In addition, Hispanic Mennonites were willing to take risks. Biblical promises were taken almost literally as the Concilio made plans. Our churches had a total of 908 members in 24 congregations in 1975. For 1982, the 50th anniversary of the first Mennonite ministry to Hispanics, we set a goal of 50 churches and 2,000 members. We reached it — doubling in size in seven years.

Achievements such as this were occasions for celebration. Often I wonder if traditional Mennonite ethics allow people to enjoy success, or even to plan for it openly in areas other than business and professions. Why? Suffering servants deserve times of rejoicing.

During my eight years with the Concilio and General Board, I felt both support and insensitivity from Anglo Mennonites. At times I felt alone in my work. Yet when I asked for help or a second opinion, my colleagues were responsive and the secretaries cooperative. Likewise, I saw people in the wider Mennonite Church open their congregations, structures and homes to Hispanics and members of other minority groups.

At the same time, I found a lack of understanding of many difficulties Hispanics face. One of these is language. Hispanics are expected to function in English, which is often their second language. Yet Anglo audiences are notoriously intolerant of speakers with foreign accents. The deep involvement of Mennonites in overseas mission and service projects has made them a bit more patient than their neighbors, but their minds still tend to wander when they listen to an Hispanic.

I also found little understanding of the financial problems with which Hispanic Mennonites must work. Hispanics as a group are not wealthy, and what they give to the church tends not to come from surplus, but at great personal cost. To cover the gap between contributions and expenses, Mennonite conferences and mission boards have provided subsidies for pastoral salaries. However, this system has created an unhealthy feeling of ownership on the part of the agencies and dependency on the part of the churches. Autonomy is impossible without financial independence.

A new generation of Hispanics is emerging with

more disposable income. Until there is enough money for the Hispanic church to be self-supporting, however, congregations need help in building up capital. That is, money from church agencies should go to build a long-term financial base, rather than to cover short-term needs.

Questions of funding were among the major sources of tension when representatives to the Concilio came together from around North America. Often we disagreed as Hispanics over how to reconcile our long-term goals with immediate financial necessity. There also were differences over the involvement of women in the church, as well as power struggles and "me first" complexes. Yet we felt the grace of God as we talked, prayed and praised the Lord, often past midnight.

In these intense, two-day meetings, we wrestled with the agenda, heard reports and shared jokes. Under the leadership of council chair Conrado Hinojosa, we learned to work together and acquired skills in making decisions. A successful pastor in Brownsville, Texas, Conrado knew what he was talking about in matters of church life and was highly respected by the Concilio representatives.

Perhaps the highlight of working for the Concilio was attending the Hispanic Mennonite conventions held every two years. A spirit of fiesta prevailed as we sang *coritos*, heard speakers and caught up on one another's lives. We discussed issues as well, from fasting and prayer to the farm workers strike organized by César Chavez in California.

Business sessions were sometimes heated, as delegates expressed impatience with church structures and their slowness to provide programs by and for Hispanics. On several occasions, senior

Anglo missionaries had a word of caution to cool off younger leaders.

But the most important function of the conventions probably was to provide encouragement and inspiration. I particularly recall the 1978 meeting, when a group came together to pray late at night in front of the Goshen College tennis courts. In the middle of the gathering knelt Héctor Muñoz, who had decided to go to Los Angeles in response to a challenge given that morning by Elías Pérez. Héctor planted three churches in southern California, before moving to Florida.

By arriving a day early at the convention sites, I was able to watch the vans come in with delegates, pastors and family members. After the last picture-taking session, I would watch the same people leave. *¡Adiós hermano, adiós hermana!*

After eight years in the office of Hispanic concerns, I also said good-bye. Thanks to the people I met, I will never be the same.

9.

Back to the Classroom

José left his church position at the end of August 1982. He did not have another job, but that was not a source of particular worry. He had just received his degree from Indiana University and was eager to start a second career in government service.

José had decided to study public administration because of his concern that "when you get too many Bible degrees you have a hard time competing in other settings. And I have felt that pastors should be able to function in and out of the pulpit." Also, government work promised more financial security and professional development than church work, as well as the chance to affect large numbers of people.

Because northern Indiana offered few opportunities for public service — and fewer still in which José's cross cultural experience was an asset — the Ortíz family rented out its house and moved to Tampa, Florida.

José could hardly have picked a worse time to look for a government job. Ronald Reagan was in his second year of office and was fulfilling his promise to slash federal spending for all programs except the military. Government agencies were cutting their work force, not adding to it.

For four months, José was unemployed. It was one of the most painful times of his life. He described the experience in a 1983 article for the independent Mennonite magazine *Festival Quarterly*:

> At the same time as the kids come for breakfast, the morning paper is delivered. The place I read first is not the headlines nor the stock market report, but the help wanted ads. After several weeks I discover that most of the jobs advertised are in the health care industry, defense technology and computers. Public administration, my new area of training, is a form of heresy for the new pharaohs in Washington, D.C. . . .
>
> The help wanted ads, the phone, the mailman and a network of friends set the agenda for the unemployed. But that is not enough. You must appear at the personnel offices and face the recruiters. After several tries one gets the feeling that the interview trail is [an endless circle]. The few jobs available are given or promised before they are fully created. The personnel office only processes the papers; the help wanted ads exist only to satisfy equal opportunity red tape.
>
> If you are turned down in three places, that is enough for one day. It is time to head for home before the traffic jam oppresses you. On the way home, you think how to answer your wife or the kids, who will ask, "How was your day?"

Looking back, José can see good as well as bad in what happened. Being without a job gave him a chance for reflection, he says. In addition, he enjoyed living in an area that had a large Hispanic population, Hispanic restaurants and grocery stores, and radio stations that broadcast in Spanish.

"Maybe the months of being unemployed were God's way of saying, 'Recharge yourself and then go back to the church,'" José says.

It was hard to be calm at the time, however. As the family's savings dwindled, José's concern deepened.

Before he had moved to Tampa, a church in Lancaster County, Pennsylvania, had invited him to be its quarter-time pastor and a quarter-time teacher at the local Spanish Mennonite Bible Institute. From the secretary of the Hispanic Concilio, José learned that the job was still available. He took it.

The Ortíz family moved to New Holland at the end of 1982. José began working at the start of the new year, and Iraida found a half-time job in town at Weaver's Poultry.

The people at the Spanish Mennonite Church of New Holland "were very good to us," José says. A group that included Juanita Santiago, who would later be José's secretary, welcomed the Ortízes when the family moved in.

Meanwhile, José had learned of an opening at Goshen College for a teacher in the Hispanic Ministries program. An outgrowth of a 1977 Mennonite Church General Assembly action on urban concerns, the program was designed to prepare students for church leadership in Hispanic settings.

José applied for the job, but he was not yet ready to give up on finding a job in government. With the knowledge of the New Holland church, he continued to apply for public positions.

In the spring of 1983, Goshen College offered José a job. He sent a letter accepting the position — only to receive a phone call later that day inviting him to interview for a job as director of Hispanic programs for the state of Pennsylvania.

"What I had prayed for came late," José says.

While the Pennsylvania invitation was not a firm offer, José believed he was a leading candidate. But he turned the interview down, along with an offer from a private firm for an administrative position serving Hispanics.

He did so for three reasons, he says: he had given his word to the college, he owned a house in Goshen and, as he puts it, "I like to teach."

Perhaps there was a fourth reason as well.

"When you work in the church for many years, as I've done, you have an investment in the church and you feel comfortable in it," he says.

Church positions offer a chance to be creative, he continues. In government work, "everything is defined by a memo. That's not how I like to operate."

Nevertheless, José admits that government work "is still a temptation" and that it took him "several years to understand the Tampa detour and the timing of God's clocks."

José joined the Hispanic Ministries program as a faculty member in 1983. He became director two years later.

Designed for current and prospective pastors, the program had two tracks. It offered a major in Hispanic Ministries as part of a bachelor's degree program, as well as a two-year certificate for students who wanted to study only in Spanish. An accredited seminary extension program was added in 1988, in association with the Seminario Bíblico Latinoamericano in San José, Costa Rica.

As director, José assumed primary responsibility to plan, staff and oversee these courses of study. In addition, he continued as an associate professor in the department. He taught classes on campus and traveled several times a year to teach weekend continuing education courses and lead short-term seminars and workshops.

In the summer of 1986, José spent five weeks in Central America as a visiting instructor under SEMILLA, a Mennonite leadership training program in the region. José visited Costa Rica, Guatemala, Honduras and Nicaragua. In each of these countries, he was impressed by his students' eagerness to learn. Some of these people were professionals who had demanding jobs, including doctors and lawyers. Others were young married couples, housewives and people with little formal education. Yet all of them gave up large chunks of their free time to improve their skills for the church.

One of José's students in Nicaragua was a 15-year-old girl. She attended José's class for six hours during the day, took high school classes in the evening and went to a trade school on Saturday. Seeing her commitment was an inspiration and a challenge, José says.

Whether in a church in Central America, an elementary school in Puerto Rico or a college classroom in the U.S. Midwest, it is the give and take with students that makes teaching worthwhile, José believes. Teachers touch the lives of their students, he continues. Students then touch the lives of other people. In this way, teaching multiplies a person's influence.

"There's no other profession like it," he says.

10.

Blooming Together

I cherish memories of my students. They are like a collage of faces carved in my memory bank. Hearing 28 third graders in Betania School in Pulguillas, Puerto Rico, singing "praises unto the Lord," taking junior high students from Academia Menonita in San Juan to La Perla, a city slum where Oscar Lewis's *La Vida* was researched, hearing about soul music from black students at Simon Kratz High School in Philadelphia and corresponding with a doctoral student from our church Sunday school—all are precious moments that don't fade away.

Teachers perform different roles in different places. At times they are prophets of the future, pointing toward utopia or proclaiming the virtues of the emerging order. At other times they are the curators of history and the defenders of tradition. In some places they are pillars of the status quo, in others catalysts for change.

Modern education has borrowed from both Hebrew and Greek models. The rabbinical schools that emerged out of the Old Testament emphasized the transfer of information from teacher to disciple. In this way, traditions were perpetuated. Today this approach is known as the "banking" system of education. Though no longer considered the ideal, it remains influential.

In Greek education, the emphasis was on dialogue between student and teacher. Teachers such as Socrates and Plato tried to nurture good relationships among teachers, students and the public. They believed that knowledge would lead to practice and to wholesome living. Of course, not all Greeks saw knowledge and morality as congruent.

Greek schools were highly regarded at the time of Christ. In fact, Greeks were so gifted in education that Greek teachers were taken as slaves or hired throughout the Roman empire.

Jesus' approach to education was more active than that of either the rabbis or the Greeks. His disciples were more than students; the New Testament term *matheses* means a follower who honors the cause of the teacher. Jesus did not merely transfer information or engage his disciples in dialogue. He taught his followers by living with them and leading them in action. He became a *dunamis*, a force by which the disciples changed their communities. Like John Koppenhaver during my Hesston College days, he was a teacher, friend and partner in learning.

Jesus' method of student recruitment was a simple "Follow me." He warned would-be dropouts that without him "nothing can be done." That radical call to discipleship produced a network of followers that turned the New Testament world upside down.

A contemporary educator who makes a similar connection between learning and daily life is Paulo Freire of Brazil, author of the book *Pedagogy of the Oppressed*. Freire urges teachers to make the student central as they plan curricula and to turn the immediate environment into a learning laboratory.

This view contrasts sharply with the colonial image of teachers as reservoirs of knowledge and the view of learning as a privilege for the elite. It also differs from the practice at many universities, where teachers lecture from "yellow pages" and are rewarded more for writing specialized articles than for quality teaching. Education for Freire, as for Jesus, is a process in which teacher and student bloom together, as they discover the liberating truth. In doing so, they find meaning for life and power to shape their history.

A biblical example of this type of learning took place near the village of Emmaus, where current events and pressing needs became the subject of a lesson for some disoriented followers of Jesus. Their journey led them to a room where they were confronted with the resurrected Lord, and empowered to become agents of reconciliation in the early church communities.

Essential to this experience was a personal encounter—"being with the Lord." Jesus' teaching approach could be described as one that emphasizes "being"—being with the people, being present-oriented, being an agent of liberation for others.

This cannot be accomplished by a computer or programmed learning system. I can't envision a descendant of Pac-Man serving as a role model for my future grandchildren, nor parents conferring with a tube about a student who has a learning disability.

Flesh-and-blood teachers, on the other hand, can have an influence that goes beyond their own lifetimes. As the Old Testament Hebrews secured immortality by having children and the Spaniards by writing books, so teachers have a sort of immortality through the ideas and examples they present to their students.

In education, teacher and student ascend the mountain of transfiguration together to see alarms and visions, then test those visions in the valleys of history. Whether on a darkening road or a radiant summit, learning occurs when teachers are alert to their students' context and seek the good of others.

11.

Talking With the Pen

Since early childhood, José has enjoyed words. Becoming a writer, however, was something that happened to him gradually, without planning.

Partly because of his speech impediment—noticeable in preaching but seldom in ordinary conversation—José "developed a taste for writing" when he was a young pastor. While serving the church at Palo Hincado, he started a newsletter called *El Relámpago*, or The Lightning Bolt. At Summit Hills, he edited *El Aquí* (Here).

As secretary for Hispanic concerns, José wrote reports so that events would be recorded, and Christian education materials to fill a gap of Anabaptist lessons and teacher's guides in Spanish. As a way to express ideas and gain credibility with Anglos, he started to write articles in English for such publications as *Mennonite Weekly Review*, based in Kansas, and *Gospel Herald*, the official magazine of the Mennonite Church.

In 1982, José became a columnist for *Festival Quarterly*. Titled "Second Sight," his column addressed such diverse issues as cultural differences, counseling, family relationships and social change. Often, he drew connections between faith and the arts, especially literature. His first piece as a regular contributor looked at Jonah, who was "overpowered and recycled" by God, and at Santiago, the fisherman in Ernest Hemingway's

The Old Man and the Sea. Later pieces included allusions to Jonathan Edwards and Nathaniel Hawthorne and analysis of a novel by statesman-writer Miguel Angel Asturias.

From some writers, references of this sort would seem like intellectual grandstanding. From José, they appear to be the natural product of a curious, far-reaching mind.

On the shelves in José's office are works of fiction, poetry, theology and sociology in both Spanish and English. His favorite writers range from the apostle Luke ("It's amazing how he even pulls out Herod and gives him a historical personality") to Nobel Prize-winning novelist Gabriel García Márquez to Spanish mystics Teresa de Jesús and Juan de la Cruz. ("In not having, it turns out that they give themselves — their souls," José says. "In their insecurity, they get what I most long for — God.")

José likes the plays of Alejandro Casonas and the ancient Greek dramatists. He enjoys the poetry of 19th century Nicaraguan Rubén Dario and that of Julia de Burgos, whose rural images remind him of his childhood. ("Sometimes I think a good night of poetry reading will do us much more good than a three-point sermon," he says.)

Though hardly a doomsayer, José laments what he sees as a general decline in interest and ability in writing. He blames part of this on the telephone.

Correspondence provides a way to sharpen writing skills, José says. Letters can spark ideas for essays and even books, and they create a historical record. Phone calls, by contrast, are shallow and fleeting.

José has reservations about the computer as well. Using a computer is too easy, he believes. Instead of writing something new, one is tempted merely to rearrange pre-existing sections.

As a part-time writer, José often wishes that he had more time to create. He would like to write about the people and places he remembers and to record the stories of the first-generation Mennonites in Puerto Rico "before they're gone." But writing on the run is far better than not writing at all, he says, noting that he works well under pressure.

According to José, his major weakness as a writer is the impatience he feels within himself—his urge to communicate a message.

"Possibly, I am in a rush to teach or indoctrinate," he says. "I don't write just for the sake of writing or to entertain. If I have to ask my readers' forgiveness, perhaps it's there."

Such apologies are unnecessary for the following piece, which remains one of José's favorites. The column first appeared in the Fall 1986 issue of *Festival Quarterly*.

12.

In Praise of Laughter

In order to protect the interests of a shipping company and its crew, the prophet Jonah was thrown into a troubled sea. Here at Goshen College, Victor Stoltzfus, the freshman president, was thrown into the Schrock Plaza fountain and asked to steer our ship to a safer course. The constituency installed him with prayers at a chapel service; the student body inaugurated him with laughter!

Laughter is a means of social engineering that brings people together regardless of sex, nationality or religion. Bill Cosby knows that. He laughs for a living and right now he is *numero uno* in show biz.

Humor used to be a way to speak of the weak, the immigrants, the less privileged. Polish jokes were abundant until a Polish priest became chief executive officer of the Vatican and a labor union leader from Gdansk won the Nobel Peace Prize. In Allentown, Pennsylvania, classmates of Lee Iacocca laughed because he enjoyed "tomato pies" but not shoofly pie. Now Mr. Iacocca laughs when he sees pizza parlors all over North America. Black preachers were often ridiculed because of their melodic preaching style and the amen corners in their churches. That changed when the press discovered that black church members give more offering money than middle-class Catholics.

In humor we expose our humanity, but as a sign of strength of the fiber of family life. One of my sons entered a neighboring university as a freshman. He dislikes reading—he is in the visual arts. Since reading poses a problem, he should have gone to Oral Roberts University, where, I was told, even the exams are—oral. Yes, we laugh at our limitations, but at times we ponder and remove our sandals.

As Mennonites, we tend to camouflage dissent. Perhaps our orientation toward consensus is why I see so many children of Menno driving Honda Accords. We claim to be a group of listeners. So are bats, elephants and rabbits, but they have king-size ears.

Family is a central theme in our churches, colleges and seminary corridors. Once I researched models of family living in Genesis and Matthew, the introductory books of the Old and New Testaments. I discovered two golden girls having babies in their golden years. I met Sarah. She said, "God made me laugh," and this barren woman gave birth to Isaac, whose name means—laughter! Elizabeth gave birth to John the Baptist in her senior years. Mary was puzzled by a teenage pregnancy while claiming virginity. At that point I held my breath. God made me laugh like Sarah!

When I go to heaven, I envision evening walks through streets named after Snoopy's friends as created by Charles Schultz. I will seek the company of the committed-to-laughter, like Cantinflas, Diplo, Cosby, Hope and other sinners. Meanwhile, I will resurrect laughter in the pulpit, in meeting places and in the classroom. Let's laugh until it hurts. It may bring tears, but both are very natural and cleansing elements of our eternal souls.

13.

Bridging Three Cultures

As an Hispanic Mennonite, José is a member of an ethnic minority inside another minority. He admits it is a challenge to be a Spanish-speaker from the Caribbean among descendants of Swiss-Germans, Russians and the Amish. Yet, he says, the difficulties are outweighed by the joys.

"Even nature has its seasons," he says. "Being exposed to different cultures brings variety, like the seasons of the year."

José finds many shared values among Anglo Mennonites and Hispanics. Both groups value family and community, he says. Also, both like to connect new acquaintances to other people they know or places they have been.

Among Mennonites, this sometimes takes the form of questions about one's relatives: Who was your father, or do you know my sister? This can be uncomfortable for people who did not grow up as Mennonites or who come from areas outside the group's population centers. But José has found his own ways of playing the game: "I say, 'I went to college with this person from this community at this time,' or 'I knew this mission worker in Puerto Rico.'

'Oh! I know that person!'"

The value placed on belonging sets both Hispanics and Anglo Mennonites apart from general North

American society, which prizes personal independence. In both groups, "the life of the individual becomes the life of a people," José says — though he notes that Mennonites are becoming less group-oriented as they move into the mainstream of society.

Likewise, the Hispanic struggle to preserve a language parallels Anglo Mennonite experience. Only in the last 100 years has English become the dominant language among Mennonites in the United States and Canada.

"Sometimes I like to floor Mennonites by speaking to them quite fast and in Spanish," José observes. "And sometimes they will answer me in German. Then we discover that we are foreigners together."

In spite of these similarities, Anglo Mennonites and Hispanics differ in major ways, José says. Mennonites enjoy planning and organizing, he notes, and are good at preserving the past. As a group, they are frugal and effective financial managers — "One time I suggested that they could run Amtrak and make a profit."

Because of their skill with money, however, Anglo Mennonites are reluctant to allow minority persons to handle church funds, José says. He sees this as a type of arrogance — "the feeling that they can be stewards of money better than anyone else."

Similarly, José finds Anglo Mennonites "very protective" of "the inner circles of decisionmaking. . . . A new work is established and Anglo Mennonites are put in control."

Anglos are slowly allowing minorities to lead, he says, "but not to the point of mutual satisfaction."

In contrast to Germanic Mennonites, who the wider society views as cold and unable to have fun, Hispanics love "to celebrate the moment, the event," José says. "We tend to be festive."

Hispanics are willing to improvise and to try, José continues. This differs from the Germanic view that "unless you can do it well, you don't do it."

Along with this, he says, Hispanics have "the freedom to express our hurts and suffering, to admit our brokenness. For us, private life is not so private."

This is particularly evident in times of death, José says. Anglo funerals tend to be "very well orchestrated." At Hispanic funerals, "people cry."

Airing grief, frustrations and anger makes it possible for people to support one another, José believes.

Finally, Hispanics "leave room for the unexpected — for surprise." Sometimes this is an excuse for poor planning or fatalism, José admits. But it recognizes God's ability to work in ways beyond human planning.

One expression of this flexibility is an emphasis on people rather than schedules, José says. If an Hispanic meets someone on the way to a meeting, he or she typically will stop to talk, "even at the expense of being late."

Anglos can learn from this, José suggests, while Hispanics can learn to become more efficient. Within the Mennonite Church, he would like to see both groups find "a balance between being spontaneous and organized." In addition, he would like Anglo Mennonites to reach out more in church growth and Hispanics to build fellowship and relief networks like those of Mennonite Disaster Service (which aids storm victims of all faiths), Mennonite Central Committee thrift shops (which support development projects around the world) and organizations of Mennonite professionals.

Hispanics, by and large, are not participating in these projects, he says.

Together, Hispanic and Anglo Mennonites have much to offer the society around them, José believes. In

Commencement day at Goshen College, Goshen, Indiana, in April 1984. With José and Iraida are José and Teresa Matamoros, originally from Costa Rica. The Matamoros couple has been involved in pastoral work in Costa Rica; Nicaragua; and San Antonio, Texas.

José talks with students from the Hispanic Ministries program in the spring of 1987. Juan Vega (far left) became pastor of Iglesia del Buen Pastor in Goshen. The other students (left to right) are: Manuel Báez, who went into video production in Tampa, Florida; Aureliano Vazquez, a church planter in Laredo, Texas; and Israel Fuentes, a pastor in Valinda, California. (Goshen College photo by J. Douglas Abromski)

José preaches at Iglesia del Buen Pastor in Goshen. "For the past 12 years our family has been ministered to and developed friendships there." (Photo by J. Douglas Abromski)

José poses with faculty member Elizabeth Soto (seated center), secretary Juanita Santiago (seated at right) and students in the Hispanic Ministries department in April 1988. (Photo by J. Douglas Abromski)

José and Iraida together in Goshen. "Iraida deserves major credit for raising three teenagers without major dents, despite our living in six states and 16 different homes [during that time]." (Photo by Juanita Santiago)

The Ortíz family, July 1989. (Photo by Juanita Santiago)

addition to technical expertise, Anglos can provide a sense of history. Their challenge, he says, is to show the relevance of 16th century Anabaptist values to the modern world.

'Anabaptist' is a term that has to be used carefully, because it is often misused," he says. "It has become a soft couch where Mennonites sit."

Nevertheless, José views the Anabaptists as a valuable model of people who lived the vision of the early church. Like the early Christians, they believed that faith must be expressed in ethical living and emphasized mutual support and discernment within the church, José observes. The Anabaptists also stressed peacemaking and love for one's enemies.

As a young man growing up in the 1940s and '50s, José found that this message of peace offered an alternative to the violent world he saw around him. Dictators ruled the Caribbean, from Trujillo in the Dominican Republic to Batista in Cuba and Duvalier in Haiti. Perón had just been ousted in Argentina.

"There was blood in those countries," José says. "There was blood in Jerusalem. Korea was bursting."

In addition, pacifism fit with the example of José's father. Patient and slow in talking, he was "not in a rush to get angry, not in a rush to make judgments, not in a rush to hurt people."

Important as peacemaking is to him, José decries Mennonites who emphasize it exclusively. Anabaptism "wasn't just peace—it was evangelism," he observes. One of the fastest-growing religious groups in history, the Anabaptists for a time seemed likely to become the leading denomination in Europe.

Hispanic Mennonites represent the evangelistic side of Anabaptism much better than Anglos do, José says. He believes that Hispanics can keep the

Anglo respect for history from becoming nostalgia or self-congratulation.

"If we cannot get new converts, that says that our faith is just a folk religion," he observes.

In addition to what they can accomplish together in a practical way, José believes that Hispanic and Anglo Mennonites could provide a model to the world of what it means to be one in Christ.

Unity does not mean the elimination of differences but an appreciation for variety, José explains. He compares it to a multi-ethnic meal, to which Pennsylvania Germans bring meat loaf, home fries and rhubarb pies; African Americans bring greens, black-eyed peas, pork and cornbread; Mexicans bring jalapeño peppers and enchiladas; and Puerto Ricans bring arroz con pollo, *plátanos* (fried plantain bananas) and *piragua* (ice cones "with natural juices").

Each group contributes a flavor of its own and adds nourishment to the dinner. When this happens, says José, who grows his own vegetables and loves to eat, the result is truly a foretaste of heaven.

14.

Home for a Wedding

My youngest sister insisted that I must come home to Puerto Rico for her wedding. It took place in 1983, the last marriage in our family of nine children.

She was the second in the family to marry within the Roman Catholic church, this time a brief ceremony, a pocketbook version of what church weddings used to be.

As usual, a Saturday morning wedding brought a traffic jam among the shoppers in the small town of Aibonito. For a person like me with a preference for solitude, driving in a caravan with dozens of cars honking horns is quite an exercise in tolerance, but I survived the 20-minute ride to my parents' home in Asomante.

The newlyweds enjoyed it all, especially the sunny, tropical morning made to order. The event was full of worship, carnival, folklore and tradition, all elements in flux in that world, as well as my own.

My parents' home was ready for the reception; in fact, Mother stayed there to assure that things were in order and on time. Maria Emilia—who carries the names of my mother and grandmother—was showered with rice as she got out of the car, a tradition that I also witnessed while traveling in

Asia. The practice expresses the wish that the couple live in a world of plenty.

People gathered in the living room for the second chapter — the cutting of the cake, the pictures, the brief speeches, the handshakes, the well-wishing. My father read from the Bible about the wedding at Cana of Galilee, a reminder that in the same way that Jesus acted when there was a shortage of wine, he will act in the many shortages of life. If we let him he will respond to our needs, just like at Cana.

I had the rare experience of stretching out my hand to a man who had just become my brother-in-law, but whom I had not met before. A handshake, a hug and a "Welcome to the family" bridged us together.

Eventually the meal, the fellowship, the well-wishing came to an end, and by mid-afternoon most of our relatives, friends and visitors headed home. Their coming for the wedding said, "We are in this together." A merger has taken place and the witnesses have become trustees for the home just born. It takes more than two to make a happy marriage.

The event also meant the conclusion of 25 years of parenting for my folks. Their nine children have become 18 children, some with unusual names such as Hershberger and Brenner, and others with more familiar names such as Lopez and Espada. None of us has more than three children; no one is rushing to break the magic number of nine!

Now the nest was empty. For the first time I saw a surplus of beds in our home — usually there was a shortage. My father and mother, just like the newlyweds, now had to face each other and explore avenues to find fulfillment in each other's company.

Let's see how they survive without the "kids" —
at times the glue that keeps couples together. The
miracle of life continues. It is a privilege to be an
eyewitness.

15.

A World of Mennonites

On a hot July evening in 1978, some 16,000 Mennonites and Brethren in Christ gathered at Cessna Stadium in Wichita, Kansas, as part of the 10th Mennonite World Conference assembly.

Never before in the 450-year history of these groups had so many members assembled in one place. As José sang with this huge congregation from 44 nations, it seemed to him that this was the largest crowd of Anabaptists he would see "on this side of heaven." As at the session the night before, when he sat beside a group of ministers from the Soviet Union, John's vision in the Book of Revelation seemed to be coming true before his eyes.

Mennonite World Conference brings together Mennonites and Brethren in Christ for fellowship and fraternal discussions. Not long before the Hispanic Concilio invited him to become associate secretary, José was appointed to the World Conference Presidium, now called the Council. As one of two representatives for Latin America, he was given the daunting task of representing churches in 19 countries, from Argentina to Mexico, and from Paraguay to Puerto Rico.

In 1976, the year the United States celebrated its bicentennial, José traveled to Semerang, Indonesia, to attend a Presidium meeting. At the airport, discarded Soviet helicopters lay like the carcasses of ducks. The scene reminded José of the U.S. experience in Vietnam.

The tropical Indonesian countryside was like that of the Caribbean. However, the crowds along the road, the row houses and the congested bus stops showed the pressures of overpopulation and poverty. Human backs, rather than heavy machinery, built the roads and harvested the sugar cane that would sweeten the desserts of affluent foreigners.

What was the good news for these people? José wondered. Would economic development programs reach them? The poor and dispossessed are a major concern of the biblical prophets, yet "here they were sweating, maybe spitting blood."

In the midst of this difficult situation, the Indonesian church was active and growing. Congregations held several services in the same building on Sunday mornings, like the movie houses. Churches reached out to their local communities through health programs, economic development projects and food programs.

The Indonesian Christians had suffered from colonial wars, political instability and economic exploitation by the Dutch, Japanese and North Americans. Yet, "the church continued to perform miracles." Christians around the world "wonder how to be faithful in the midst of change, and how to distinguish between the gospel and Western culture," José says. "The Indonesians I saw were doing both."

José was impressed by the Indonesians' reverence for time and people. They did not demand quick answers to eternal questions but expressed their faith through silence. Spiritual commitments in the West are often like mushrooms, which sprout quickly but soon fade, José says. For the Indonesians, "faith was not a disposable item but an experience to be cherished and patiently nurtured."

79

On the way home from Semerang, José stopped in Japan for five days in order to visit Mennonite churches on the northern island of Hokkaido. He had "an uneasy feeling" when he arrived at the Sapporo airport and no one was there to meet him. But, with the help of a dictionary, an airport assistant gave him instructions on how to catch a downtown bus, get a train and hail a taxi in order to get to his destination.

As the bus rolled into town, he felt both faith and worry. "Like Corrie Ten Boom in *The Hiding Place,* I believed that a miracle would take place," José wrote later. "Yet, a part of me doubted."

· A "We speak English" sign in a bank caught his attention. While exchanging dollars for yen, one of the bank managers overheard his conversation with the teller and offered to help. He went with José to the subway, bought two tokens and rode with him on two trains. Then he translated the address José had into Japanese characters and instructed him to get out at the last stop.

"When everybody else got out, I did the same," José recalls. "I handed my note to a white-gloved taxi driver. He started the car and through the radio came the voice of Nat King Cole, a black American artist, singing a song in Spanish! In less than ten minutes, I was at the home of my missionary host. The Japanese were gracious to me and the Lord was faithful, but at times I trembled."

Because he had moved to North America, José was not eligible for reappointment to the Presidum after his first term expired in 1978. As a result, he says, he had to leave just when he was beginning to feel comfortable in his position.

José notes that the 1976 meeting and a 1975 missions consultation in Puerto Rico came while he was trying to learn his job as secretary for Hispanic concerns. Further, his office in Illinois was next door to that of executive secretary Paul Kraybill, so he was sometimes hesitant to speak in World Conference meetings for fear of seeming to undercut his colleague.

Coming to the Presidium was "like playing in the major leagues," José says, or "being named to the sacred College of Cardinals." Yet here, as in his work with the General Board, "active leadership was discouraged in favor of the 'servant leader' model. Using power openly, or even admitting that you had it, was seen as an expression of heresy."

Leaders of emerging churches sometimes found this approach confusing, José says. During his term on the Presidium, however, they tended to defer to their wealthier and more experienced counterparts from North America and Europe.

This is likely to change, José believes. In 1978, some 40 countries had Mennonite church bodies. By 1988, that number has risen to nearly 60, with a total membership of more than 800,000. Soon Mennonites from what Kraybill calls "the two-thirds world" will have the numerical majority. In addition, José notes, they will have greater language skills than the North Americans and will be used to moving cross culturally and ecumenically.

This will have implications not just for leadership style but on a wide range of church issues, José believes. Meetings will be less business oriented and focus more on the search for "spiritual affinity through the ministry of the Holy Spirit." Church programs may be designed more economically. At the same time, budgets may include an element of faith—trusting that God will provide funds above the amount that could otherwise be expected.

81

Of all the issues facing the global Mennonite church, José believes, perhaps the most basic is how to speak of Christ in terms and symbols that transcend culture. "A Jesus who can't cross cultural barriers is a creation of folklore, myth or unfulfilled fantasies," José says, "not the biblical messiah." Whether in the Philippines or Pennsylvania, Japan or Germany, "we must be prepared to experience pentecost at our meeting tables and church gatherings as we celebrate the commonality of the cross."

16.
Faith and Frontiers

Compared with other world religions the Christian faith has often been the prophet of the future. It also has been the guardian of the past and its many traditions. At times Christians have been caught without knowing whether to look forward or back, much like the Israelites in the wilderness: at some times they hoped for the promised land, at others they thought of what they had left behind in Egypt.

As the Israelites remembered "melons, garlic, the pots of meat and the cucumbers," so I sometimes think nostalgically of my upbringing in Puerto Rico. I recall the almond-colored faces, the feasts and the family networks. Even the poverty can be romanticized in my mind, amid the stresses of my current life.

People have always looked at the frontier, the unknown, with both fear and fascination. For Galileo, the heavens invited study and discovery, but the church would not tolerate his idea that the sun was the center of the universe, instead of the earth. That theory upset accepted theology. Science put him in the textbooks; religion placed him in limbo.

In the '60s and '70s, some people said that humankind should stay on the good earth, but astronauts left their footprints on the moon and dared to read the Bible from lunar orbit. Now, terms like "black holes" and the "Big Bang theory" are being incorporated into everyday language.

Science is reaching in as well as out. Genetic engineering is becoming a major industry. Human conception is taking place outside the human body.

We are programming how and when to give birth and when and how to die — choices earlier reserved for God. Human beings have lived for months with a pumping device instead of a heart. Cloning, or making carbon copies of animals and even people, is a goal of some scientists.

There is talk of venturing into our genetic codes to modify our DNA (heredity bank) in order to remove the bug that produces destructive behavior. In the process, we could be tempted to plan the creation of a super race, like Nietzsche and Hitler did.

In the midst of rapid change, old symbols of faith must be supplemented by new ones. "The Lord is my shepherd" makes little sense to an urban commuter who has never seen sheep. In the same way that the images of Psalm 23 are taken from everyday life at the time of David, Christians today need to adopt symbols from the world around them. Perhaps affluent city-dwellers could say "The Lord is my consultant."

Different symbols are needed for different cultures as well as different times. The New Jerusalem in the Book of Revelation is described in terms of thrones, gates, trumpets and banquets — symbols quite repulsive to colonized peoples.

While the Bible's message is eternal, its language is not. I respect Christian writers who try to explain their faith without traditional symbols or religious cliches. It is wrong to rush to judgment of these people, or to label their ideas as heretical simply because they are expressed in unfamiliar terms.

Important as they are, words alone will never adequately describe a transcendent God. For this reason, "the word became flesh and dwelt among us." In addition, God spoke audiovisually, through visions.

Today, television and video provide new means of spreading the Gospel. As the scandals involving Jim and Tammy Bakker and Jimmy Swaggart show, however, the electronic media must be used with great care.

Computers pose further opportunities and dangers. Compu-worship, a combination of the silicon chip and cheap grace, could be something waiting for us in the future.

It will not always be easy to see the difference between creative adaptations to culture and gimmicks that either trivialize or compromise the Christian message. Should a church offer spaghetti dinners to attract people to midweek services? Is it appropriate to entertain children with puppets? To hold video worship services? How about stress management lectures for adults? Offering Bible or other courses for college credit?

Not every method of attracting people is appropriate. The church could become utilitarian in purpose and de-emphasize worship, but then it would lose its identity and reason for being. Instead, the church needs to become less colonialistic and more community based. In this way, the church of the future will meet its past.

In the Lord's Supper, "in remembrance of me" and "until we meet again" merge with Christ at the center. The paradox is like Salvador Dali's master-piece *The Crucifixion*, in which Christ is suspended from the cross, free from time and space, yet the center of history in whom history finds its meaning.

17.
Facing the Future

As he enters his fifties, José looks ahead to late middle age with a mixture of gratitude and concern. His children have become young men—Rolando married and a production manager at a Goshen factory, Ricardo a university art student and Ronaldo a senior in high school and president of his church youth group. Soon José and Iraida will face the empty nest.

Professionally, José says he enjoys teaching and college administration. Yet he would like to run something larger than his department—perhaps in government or business. If he is to make a move, he will have to do it soon, he believes. Before long, he will face age prejudice as well as ethnic barriers.

Growing older also has brought questions about retirement and reflections about death. One of José's brothers, José Luis, died in 1982, shortly after José had returned to Goshen from a trip to Puerto Rico. Though he had visited his brother in the hospital a few days earlier, José's inability to be present for the funeral added to his grief.

In 1986, just two months after one of his nephews had drowned in a pool, José's mother died of a heart attack. José cut short a visit to Pennsylvania and flew home for the funeral. A year later, Iraida made a similar journey when her mother was dying.

"Death sets us apart, and death brings us together,"

José says. While the passing of a loved one leaves a gap in a family's life, it can pull the survivors together in mutual support, he believes.

José regrets that his sons have not shared in the experience of burying a family member. In order to "equip them to cope with death and dying," he and Iraida have urged them to attend funerals within the church and the local community.

As he reflects on the remaining years of his life, José struggles with the question of where to locate. Should he retire in Puerto Rico, close to his roots but far from his children? He is determined to stay out of a nursing home. Soberly, he has pondered the "reality of aging, without much capital, in a foreign land with a higher and higher cost of living and medical expenses."

In addition to such personal concerns, José is troubled by the widening gap between rich and poor in the society around him and by trends with his denomination. In many areas of life, he sees Mennonites adopting the values of their neighbors—"disposing of the devil in theology," drinking alcohol, getting divorced, driving expensive cars and contributing less than 5 percent of their income to the church.

But José is hardly given to despair. "I am enthusiastic about the future," he says. "If we Christians don't bring optimism to life, no one will."

Along with problems, José continues to find signs of hope. Hispanics are gaining influence in politics, business and the arts. Along with this will come a reassessment of the Hispanic role in North American history, he believes. (The Spanish came to Florida 100 years before the *Mayflower* landed, José points out.) In the Mennonite church, he sees a new crop of Anglo leaders emerging—"more cosmopolitan, open to the larger world."

Closer to home, José has found great joy in the growth of his sons. All three are involved, to varying extents, in the church. Of the children, Rolando had felt the most distance from his parents' values, and José and Iraida worried for a time about his participation in a rock band. After the band's breakup, however, he turned his attention to contemporary Christian music and to recording music for church videos. He was married at Good Shepherd Mennonite Church and attends there frequently with his wife, Daniela (Vukosavljevic), who comes from Serbian Orthodox background.

Ricardo, two years younger than Rolando, lives in an area where there is no Hispanic Mennonite congregation. But he participated regularly in church activities before leaving home. Skilled in painting, ceramics and woodworking, he has a learning disability but compensates with what José calls "a very sharp memory."

Ronaldo, the youngest, has the strongest church ties, José says. In addition to serving as president of his youth group, he has attended Hispanic church meetings with his father.

"I feel privileged to have raised a family that was not an embarrassment to me in my ministry," José says. "It wasn't the perfect home, but I give credit to my wife for helping those kids to grow and being there when I was absent."

José admits that his work schedule and frequent relocations have hampered family life. In 26 years of marriage, he and Iraida have moved more than 20 times.

"She has resented that," he admits. "And she has resented my being out of the home."

As the Ortíz children become fully independent, José hopes Iraida will take more leadership in church and community activities. She was very active in the church before the children were born, he says, but has preferred to remain in the background since.

"In that sense she is very Puerto Rican," he says. "Her main role is to be a mother and to be a wife — for the time being."

Perhaps because of this, Iraida, he says, has been less troubled than he has by the financial sacrifice involved in church work. Though careful in her use of money, she is seldom anxious about financial matters. José, by contrast, says he is "what you call in the States 'a child of the Depression.'"

He recalls visiting an insurance company when he was in his late forties and being asked what his net worth was. "I felt like a loser," he says.

Without a large savings account or investments, José relies on careful budgeting and "trust in the Lord. So far, it hasn't failed."

What he has lacked in money has been offset to a large extent by friendships, he continues. José has friends in at least half of the 50 states. He calls these relationships his "biggest accumulation of wealth."

Along with learning to know others, José says that over the years he has become more confident in himself and in what he has to offer to the Mennonite church.

At first, "I thought of myself as a second-class citizen with a second-class language," he observes. "Now, I'm not arrogant, but I'm saying that my ideas and experience are as good as those of anyone else. The way the Mennonite church will go, good or bad, I am responsible."

In the past, minority persons pleaded for a role in the church. In the future, they will expect it as their due, José says. Other Mennonites will hardly be in a position to refuse, he continues, noting that black and Hispanic congregations are growing while many white churches are stagnating.

The transition to multiculturalism will be painful, he predicts, especially for white Mennonites. But the result will be a stronger and healthier church.

"I'm excited that the Mennonite church will have the participation of people of all races," he says.

Such a body will attack the spiritual roots of social problems, including drug abuse, he believes. Instead of simply telling people to say no, it will invite them to a way of life in which drugs are unnecessary.

Such a church will bring together evangelism, family issues and justice, José continues. It will bring a social concern to business, as the Mennonite Economic Development Association is already doing through meetings, newsletters and investment projects.

Inevitably, the Mennonite church of the future will fall short of some of its goals, José says. But he notes that "in baseball, if you get three or four hits in 10 times at bat, you're a champion. We're going to fail in some areas, but here and there we'll get a hit."

José admits he is unsure how best to fit into the church's effort — as a teacher, full-time pastor or active member with responsibilities in both the congregation and the world around him.

"I'd like to take a crack at managing something or making a program run in secular society — but not at the expense of my ministry," he says.

Whatever he does, José has clear ideas about how he'd like to be remembered. He wants to be known as someone who treated people fairly, paid his bills and "helped to make things happen, not because of our resources but because of our enthusiasm and spirit."

More specifically, he wants to be remembered "as a person who brought people together. . . . Something happens when people meet that is God-given.

"If I fail in my dealings with people, perhaps it's in

91

giving them the benefit of the doubt," he adds. "I like to invest in people."

About the Authors

José Ortíz is director of the Department of Hispanic Ministries at Goshen College, Goshen, Indiana. He is the author of *iVen! Camina con Nosotros* (Come, Walk With Us), a study book about Anabaptist-Mennonite beliefs.

David Graybill is a magazine and book editor from Lancaster, Pennsylvania. He is a 1978 graduate of Goshen College and holds a master's degree in English from the University of Virginia.